Land Acquisition in India

Is the farmer wrong...?

KARAN DOSHI

To my Granduncle, Arun Doshi, whose practical approach to land dealings should be an inspiration to us all...

Table of Contents

1. Introduction

Land; its purchase, sale, acquisition, development etc. are all events that are invariably accompanied by strong sentiments, emotions, feelings of entitlement, in addition of course to monetary considerations. A touchy subject for most, especially when land is being acquired 'forcibly'... A subject that may draw much loathing, the general view being that land is being taken away from the pitiable land owner, the ill-fated farmer is being harassed by the greedy political or the builder / industrialist lobby. Utterances like 'if I had the power, I would ban land acquisition altogether' or 'I feel for that poor owner whose land got taken away' and so on are commonplace...

Well, in this book, I would like to provide an alternate view point, a new way of looking at things, a somewhat different perspective, something I strongly believe is of the utmost importance and something that currently hardly finds any place in our thoughts, or views, or gets portrayed in the media, or receives any sound bites in our debates or is barely even registered in our collective conscious. Further, what specifically got me to pen this book is the introduction, by our current Government (i.e. the Indian Govt.; I am an Indian citizen) led by

PM Narendra Modi, of a Bill. The Bill is titled 'The Right to Fair Compensation and Transparency in Land Acquisition, Rehabilitation and Resettlement (Amendment) Bill, 2015' [1]. This Bill amends the similarly named Act of 2013 [2]. As can be inferred from the title itself; this Bill deals with land, primarily its acquisition for development purposes. Expectedly, emotions run high on both sides as it is concerned with that one asset we hold most dear...

Now, I guess the reader will be expecting me to give a detailed analysis of this Bill. To give you the bad news or rather the good news, as I am sure no one wants a rather long drawn technical conversation on the law, I will Not debate this proposed Amendment Bill. I will not be vetting it clause by clause, weighing the pros and cons of each section and then coming to my conclusions, suggestions etc. This is not what I have in mind. Rather than weighing the fine points of the current Bill, I want to focus on something far more basic, something that I will call the 'concept of land'...

This concept relates to what is meant by land, it's ownership, it's acquisition, sale, redevelopment etc. which invariably give rise to strong emotions, feelings of entitlement, bonds of attachment and of course monetary expectations. Are these emotions justified? The reader could well argue as to who indeed am I to comment on emotions... Isn't it supposed to be a personal notion? What will I criticize next, your choice of dress? Well of course, no... However, what is to be realized is that a good part of our thoughts, feelings, preferences are made up of our life experiences which further depend on the environment in which we grew up, our education, our family values, our culture etc. For e.g. a woman who has been brought up in the Middle East may, well, willingly wear a 'Burkha', even prefer it, as that's what she's worn throughout her adult life, and that's what she's seen everyone from her mother, sisters, female friends and relatives wearing. It probably becomes so ingrained in her as to seem perfectly natural. Alternatively, a woman living in the US or Europe would recoil at the very thought.

Similarly for this case too, and with apologies for sounding pompous, I would like to take the role of showing us all, the 'Burkha' clad woman, an alternate possible way of life and thought. This alternate thought process, in my firm opinion, being far more rational, logical and ultimately far more suitable for our nation's continued growth and prosperity. Further, as will be eventually argued, essential for our very survival itself...

In the remainder of this book, I will base my arguments on the assumption that if land is indeed acquired, that a fair price is paid for it; whether it is the Govt. acquiring land for public infrastructure projects or even a builder who wants to take over your flat / apartment for redevelopment; you are being duly compensated...

With this caveat and an important one at that, I take the firm the stand that if land acquisition is being done for the greater common good like

- for public infrastructure projects say railways, airports, roads etc.

- or for setting up of industries

- or as part of a development of an entire area say from slums to housing complexes

- or even if it is your old house going in for redevelopment

- and again I repeat this, that you are being duly compensated

then with a smiling face, one should say 'Yes'...

2. Impossibility of development without a contiguous piece of land...

Few people will disagree that development is important... Let us try and understand that word; 'development'. What images get conjured up in our minds when we use that term? A few things that come to mine are listed below; in no particular order

- Industries

- Airports

- Railways

- Roadways

- Harbors

- Dams

- Planned Cities housing the millions of our aspiring middle class in comfortable and dignified accommodation etc.

Now, I will forcibly argue that for any of these projects, a large and contiguous piece of land is required... Shouldn't land owners, whether they are farmers or residential flat owners or whosoever in the greater interest of national development and as earlier stated if duly compensated willingly give up their land. I say, yes... Let us take each of the items listed above and discuss...

Industries: The backbone of a strong and economically vibrant society. The big scale ones and even the smaller ones need a contiguous piece of land. Imagine a factory split in two, because some uncompromising farmer wouldn't part with his land, in which half the work is done at one place before the semi finished goods are loaded into trucks and then moved to the other half for further processing. Silly, impractical but more importantly inefficient as it would incur pointless costs making our products less competitive...

Airports: Imagine a farmer whose land is smack in the middle of a runway and he refuses to give it up. The runway gets split in two. What are planes to do? Land on half a runway, then take-off and land back on the other half; laughable...

Railways: The train halts where the track ends on some farmer's land who hasn't relinquished his right. Then all passengers alight with their luggage and board a new train waiting on the other side and the track continues. Silly, you'll say...

Now, one possible counterargument is that we bend the rail line to bypass the land. Yes, possible but mind you a rail line cannot be bent by more than a specific amount or the train risks danger of derailment. Plus the roundabout way increases rail length, takes longer and costs more to both build and run. Do also note that high speed trains, running in quite a few countries now and planned to be introduced in ours, do require a straight path with minimum bends... Plus, no guarantees that on that new bent patch some other farmer would not refuse to sell...

Roads: A similar reasoning to railways can be applied but with the caveat that roads do offer greater flexibility. However, the author prefers the American style of straight and true roads rather than a continuous twisting and turning one...

Now, the main thrust in these arguments is that a contiguous piece of land is indeed required for any major, or even minor, infrastructure projects. This may seem obvious to the reader... Of course, I get it that half a runway is useless; you think I am a dim wit not to get this; the reader may irately claim. I agree and I myself prefer not to give such childish reasons... But do realize that this is indeed what is happening... A case in point: When the Mumbai Pune Expressway was being built, a plot of land owned by one Mr. Nanikram Devnani was located smack in the middle of the Expressway [3]... Now, said Devnani refused to part with it and the matter was litigated in the Bombay High Court wherein his case was dismissed by a bench comprising the Hon'ble

Palshikar (acting Chief Justice) and Hon'ble Bhosale being Writ Petition WP/10/1997 [4]. The point here being that this is indeed what is happening and further that in a majority of instances, the matter doesn't even reach the Courts; the landowners resorting to agitation, 'dharnas', even rioting and other extra Judicial ways resulting, in many cases, in the government cancelling the entire project altogether...

Harbor: If the sea bed is conducive for a harbor with a deep sea floor and flat bottom then yes; it should be made. What if the fishermen don't agree to part with their land next to the shore? Most of the major cities of the world including my city of Mumbai (erstwhile known as Bombay) have developed because of excellent harbor facilities that the geography naturally provided. Now imagine a fisherman community refusing to budge and the British then abandoning their plans to build a harbor, India would lose its most economically vibrant city... What a loss...

Dams: Yes, the backwaters of a dam have to form a lake which sometimes covers many square kilometers. The farmer, duly compensated should relocate... The farm area that gets irrigated because of the Dam is much much larger than the area that gets submerged by the lake that forms with the net result being that far more farmers get benefited. For e.g., the whole of Punjab (our Green revolution) got a secure and perennial supply of water thanks to the Bhakra Nangal Dam [5]. Not to mention an added advantage of electricity generation... Millions in our country do not even access to this most basic of resource; electricity. Forget high-end development, electricity is required to achieve a bare minimum standard of living.

Planned Cities: We need planned cities, not only to house the millions of Indians who will be looking for housing in the coming years, but also to achieve a pleasing look that comes with a planned city. Each individual building going in for redevelopment, albeit a start, is not the ideal way going forward. The number of people getting housing does increase but there is no corresponding increase in say, the water supply, municipal services, road width to accommodate this increase in population. Entire suburbs, entire cities will have to be built from scratch to sustain a positive and enriching environment for our future generations. For private builders of today it is almost impossible to acquire 100 acre contiguous piece of land for planned development. If development does not take place in a planned and organized manner involving large tracts of land being simultaneously developed, this country will face increasing problems of urban sprawl, a preponderance of slums, disorganized housing developments, wherein basic infrastructure facilities like roads etc. are still at the pre-development level. As a side note, I recently came across an article in the newspaper of a proposal to set up an IIT or equivalent educational institute near Pune. The very next day, the local farmers protested against this project [6] and the project most probably stands scrapped. A step backward and a big loss, I state...

The key question to be answered is; have ever any reasonably big grouping of people agreed 100% on everything? Of course not... Ergo, I ask the reader an open ended question? If the idea is to not force someone off his land, trust me, none on the above enumerated list will ever get built. In no big grouping will there be unanimous agreement. A few dissenting farmers can ruin the entire project. Wherever you go, to set up your airport or railway or whatever, somewhere, someone will cause a fuss. If you're planning to get everyone on board then don't even bother trying. Won't happen... Stay at home and watch on TV how our country lags behind others...

3. Ab-initio definition of development and should the farmer be put on a pedestal...

In this section the author proposes to give an ab-initio definition of what 'development' means and then get to grips with the conclusions that follow once we understand this concept. FYI, ab-initio is Latin for 'from first principles'...

To get to our definition, we will have to look at our history as a species and rewind back to the very beginning of time. Modern humans, i.e. we all, evolved from our more primitive ape like ancestors around two hundred thousand years ago [7]. The technical term scientists use to describe our species is 'homo sapiens sapiens' [7]. The initial life style of our remote ancestors was based on a nomadic life colloquially known as 'hunter-gatherers'. Eating fruits and berries from the trees in the jungle and occasionally going on hunting sprees to kill big game [7]... Such a life is the original, the ab-initio and the natural state of existence of man and one could conclude in harmony with nature, long before cities and civilization and our present modern world. Thus and this is the crucial point, anything on a superior level to a hunter-gatherer existence is development.

Today we are so far removed from this existence that we find it hard to relate to our original way of life, but in fact the majority of our existence as a species on this planet has been precisely lived this way. To give you some figures, modern humans, as stated earlier, evolved around two hundred thousand years ago from our more primitive ape-like ancestors and for the next one hundred and ninety two thousand years or so we have lived as hunter-gatherers. Only in the last approximately eight thousand years or so did we take the first steps towards development and to modern civilization [7].

This first step, or in Neil Armstrong's words "a giant leap for mankind", being the invention of agriculture around eight thousand years ago [7]... It may hardly seem like high technology today but the process of laying the seed, to tilling the land, watering it, removing of weeds, harvesting and so on; in short the entire process starting from the seed to the fruit is an example of man applying a technology called agriculture. It is an industrial process, though hardly referred to in that way, which takes raw materials and turns them into a finished goods using the industry called farming and a technology called agriculture. This technological innovation represents a major leap forward in human progress. From wanderers, we settled down to grow crops, which then developed into villages, the villages into small towns and so on to the pinnacle of modern civilization of today.

Of course, land in the present time is used not just for the 'industry' called agriculture but for many other industries involved in manufacturing all the necessities of everyday life. We had to build roads once cars were invented, airports for airplanes, railways for trains, harbors for ships and so on. At almost every step of our development, land has played a crucial role, it being put to the use we want, being crucial to our progress and this is the important point to grasp, the farmers were our original 'industrialists'.

I, therefore, hold industrialists in high regard. Yes their primary aim is that of maximizing profit but equally essential is their role of converting low value goods to high value finished products creating wealth on which depends the very existence of our modern way of life. So, let's not hate our entrepreneurs, our industrialists, our businessmen and if we do hate them, then equally hate our 'industrialist' farmers as well. Further, let's not put farmers on some sort of a pedestal. That they contribute to society by producing food is given, but so do other industries by producing other finished goods we need in our daily lives...

In any argument it has become the de-facto if not the de-jure stand of claiming righteousness by saying that this is against the farmer and so shouldn't be done. What if it is against industry, well that's OK... To me this is favoritism and discrimination that will slow our march towards progress. Let us do something that does not favor any one particular group but is in the greater interest of our nation. For development and to sustain a way of life to which many of us our accustomed, we need all; the new mantra being '*Jai Jawan, Jai Kisan and Jai Businessman*'.

For our continued development and we do have a long way to go before we catch up with Westerns standards of prosperity, we need our businessmen and our industrialists. For those who despise industrialists and are supposedly pro-farmer please find my rejoinder below:

- Farming is an invention and a technology whose practice should, but is not called an industry. Thus, this not about taking sides in a debate representing two different entities; the farmer or the industrialist, but it now reduces to the silly notion of those being pro-farmer supporting one form of industry at the expense of the other. I cannot find any justifiable moral ground for this. Just like we need the farmers, we need modern amenities too. Any life the reader can imagine that does not involve just growing crops or living in the jungle needs other industries, big and small. Your TV, car, refrigerator, airplane, to life saving drugs, to even the simple light bulb, all come from an industry other than agriculture. Encourage it...

- One argument is that Industries harm the environment. Well, if they are within the environmental regulatory framework and their pollution levels are monitored and found within prescribed norms, then this is a price one must be willing to accept or else let's forgo our aforementioned creature comforts. Further Note this; the perception that farming or agriculture does not pollute is plain wrong. The farmer who cleared a forest to grow crops is the first and the biggest reason for environmental degradation on planet Earth. A forest of trees is far more environmentally friendly than an equivalent crop planted in its place after cutting those trees. The original trees release more oxygen to the environment, have better nutrient holding capacity, contribute greater to biodiversity, better resistance to drought, have a superior nutrient exchange capacity amongst many other advantages [8]. Further, trees by virtue of their superior green cover for the same area contribute better to the various cycles of oxygen, nitrogen, phosphorous, carbon etc. which are crucial for sustaining life on our planet.

More recently the past century or so (and yes, when talking about an age old industry like farming even a hundred years can be considered relatively recent) has seen the introduction of chemical fertilizers like ammonium nitrate, urea etc. and pesticides like DDT which the farmer of today uses liberally to increase crop yield and protect from pests... Do note that these chemicals are harmful for the environment too and are quite toxic to the human body. They get absorbed by the plants and eventually get into the fruits and vegetables. Some of it gets soaked up in the soil from where it is leached into the ground water. The essential point here is that farming is also an industry that pollutes... Further, precious little is done in our country to control this toxic brew... Most countries for e.g. have banned DDT while we still go about it as if it's business as usual [9]... To the reader, I state confidently that the adage 'Farmer; the polluter' is not an oxymoron.

• The original illegal land encroacher / grabber. The cliché is that land belongs to the farmer and the big corporations are here to take them away. Go back far enough in history and the same farmer settled on an unoccupied piece of land, claimed it to be his, chopped the forest on said claim and used it for his purpose. Land originally, going far back enough in time in whichever in part of the world you go to, belonged to Mother Nature. Without those first farmers a.k.a. industrialists a.k.a. entrepreneurs there would be no agriculture today, no crops, no vegetables etc. Those who oppose the modern day industrialists while supporting the farmers are making the mistake of assuming that the farmer has some God given right to land. To me this is double standards; when the farmer does it, it is OK but when a modern day entrepreneur acquires land and that too after compensating the farmer, that somehow becomes evil...

So, let's not look at our Industrialists / Entrepreneurs / Developers with such hatred. For our continued development going forward and we do have a long way to go before we catch up with Westerns standards of prosperity, we need them...

4. Dragons of Eden

Why are we so touchy about land? I strongly believe that it has something to do with our evolutionary past. To give the uninitiated a quick review, life on our planet evolved around four billion years ago as simple molecules that could reproduce or make copies of themselves [10]. From then on evolution has led us to more complex and sophisticated forms of life, the end result being, we get to see today the incredible diversity of plant and animal life found around us; including us humans of course [10]. I recommend an excellent book written by the famous scientist and literary, Carl Sagan, the title of which is 'Dragons of Eden'; the same title being used for this section [11]. It is a brilliant book that explains in layman's terms the concepts of evolution sans much technical jargon so as to be understood by all...

Using the theory of evolution along with fossilized evidence, it has been established that humans evolved from our 'monkey-like' primate ancestors who lived from hundreds of thousands to millions of years ago in the jungles of Africa. Going even further back, primates themselves have evolved from simple mammals similar to the modern rat. If we were to go even further back in time, we get to the reptiles and so on till the evolution of a single cell and before that to something even simpler; the first complex biological molecule able to reproduce representing the birth of life on our planet [10].

Now, as is true for every part of our body, evolution has shaped our brains too. Believe it or not, our human brain can generally be split into three different sections or parts based on our evolutionary history [12].

The first part is called the R-complex, short for Reptilian Complex. It is the first part of our brain to evolve in our remote reptilian ancestors. This part of our brain, we share with lizards, crocodiles, alligators etc. It is responsible for our basic instinctive behavior like that of territoriality, aggression, dominance and the desire to hoard resources [12]. This part of our brain makes spontaneous responses without 'thinking'. Someone is trying to occupy your sweet spot near a watering hole, someone is encroaching on your territory, someone is making a pass at your woman and immediately aggression kicks in. Without 'conscious' thought we rise to the occasion to defend to our utmost what we believe to be ours. I'm sure that all of us at some level can relate to this... This basic behavior is shared by almost all animals as they all have their own R-complexes. The reader is encouraged to watch animal documentaries on Discovery Channel or Animal Planet.

The next part of our brain that evolved and which we share with our mammalian ancestors is called the Paleomammalian complex. It is the seat of love, affection and maternal care [12]...

The final part which evolved mainly in us humans is the Neomammalian complex or commonly referred to as the Neocortex. It is the seat of logic, critical thought and reasoning [12]. This part of our brain is unique to humans and a few of our primate cousins like chimpanzees, gorillas etc., it being most advanced in us. It is this part that distinguishes us from the rest of the animal world and vide effective use of which propelled us from the jungles of Africa to the height of modern civilization and technology that we see around us today.

The reader must be wondering, what has all this go to be with land. A lot actually... Whenever the topic of land is raised, it is the ancient R-complex of our brain that gets activated. Remember that it is this R-complex that is responsible for territoriality and aggression. The result being we tend to give spontaneous responses without using logic or reason, we tend to take uncompromising positions, with our seat of logic, the neo-cortex being virtually sidelined.

There is this constant struggle in our brains between its newer and the older parts. The R-complex makes us all get emotional and aggressive and protective when this topic of 'land' comes up. Been there, done that, haven't we all...

The main thrust in this section is to make the reader realize that what suited our reptilian ancestors of millions of year past and which is still active in us does not necessarily suit us today. The reader is encouraged to recognize this particular short coming and, although extremely difficult at times, let the logical part of our brain guide us.

It is restated here that if the land being acquired is used for setting up industries, for setting up infrastructure projects for the greater good of all and if we are duly compensated, please let go. Take the money and buy something somewhere else. Let the possessiveness and territoriality go. It is detrimental to the future development of our nation and in the long run will lead to a stagnation of sorts.

Ask an accountant and he will tell you land is an 'asset' entry in the balance sheet. Well so is a car, a TV, a refrigerator, furniture etc. and so is well, a mobile phone. How many times have we changed our phones now? Do we get the same feelings of aggressiveness or anger when we buy / sell our phone? Our R-complex evolved at a time many millions of years ago when there were no mobile phones or other modern day assets. Therefore, it does not get activated when we talk of selling phones and such and we let our neo cortex take the decision based on sound reasoning. Aggression, possessiveness hardly plays a role here. Logically, the same should also hold true including for that asset called land, shouldn't it? Thus I say to thee; ban the R-complex my friends so as to avoid making emotionally charged decisions which may well be substandard to both you and society.

In the same vein and on a related topic, If there are disputes in the family and the family members are not happy living together let the patriarch sell his house and buy, say, two new smaller ones and adjust his squabbling children in them so that each can have an independent life. Love the family members and not the four walls that make up a house. Keep aside the faulty emotions emanating from the R-complex and make practical decisions. If not, there is a good chance that your heirs will fight amongst themselves post your demise. The maximum number of cases pending before our courts and there are a heck of a lot of these, are property disputes. Your listening to your R-complex and loving the 'house' rather than the family members and not taking practical decisions of separation especially if there are disputes or even minor disagreements which could very well turn into full blown disputes later, is, to me, an implied insult to the higher more evolved portions of your brain. You are made a human being, with the largest brain size amongst all animals, with capacity for practical and logical and reasoned thought; use it...

5. The Ebb and flow of life

I, though not just because I am a Hindu, do believe in concept of 'maya' [13], of us being ethereal beings. Nothing is permanent; we are here today, gone tomorrow... Without dragging much of religious connotations to this debate, all I will state is that I find this concept appealing and I do believe in its essence which is that we should not get too attached or too involved in our worldly belongings.

I have seen and I state this only from personal experience that many a time the most strongly religious amongst us, who arguably should be well versed with the concept of 'maya' are the most strongly possessive of their assets, chief among them their property. This is just an observation... I do not have any statistical evidence to prove this and even if wrong, it does not affect the overall idea being developed. To avoid, as I have stated, religious connotations to this debate, let us use the universally acceptable language of logic and reasoning to develop this point.

Say you, the reader, are an owner of a piece of land. It can be an apartment, a bungalow, a plot or whatever piece and parcel of land you own. Today it belongs to you... Probably some time back it belonged to your father, before that say your grandfather and so on. But what is inescapably true is that going sufficiently back in time you'll realize that at some point of time it belonged to someone else, some third party not among your forefathers. Your some distant relative bought it from that same third party. Now imagine that 'someone' is just as attached and just as unwilling to part. You wouldn't have that house today or piece of land, would you? What we get so very sentimental about as being ours, going sufficiently back in time did not belong to us and going sufficiently forward in time again will not belong to us either. In the going forward case, I mean not belonging to any of our forthcoming progeny. Someone somewhere down in our family tree will be a willing seller just as someone somewhere in our ancestral past was a willing buyer. What, therefore are we to make of this? I would like to inculcate the viewpoint that we are short term caretakers of land. This land has existed for thousands, no millions, no in fact billions of years. The age of the Earth is roughly four billion years and it will exist for another three and a half billion years more before being devoured by our Sun. Modern humans have roamed this planet for approximately two hundred thousand years [7]. Do a calculation as to the length of time you've occupied this piece of land to that of human existence or that of the Earth's existence. It will be much less than even 1% of that time. Natural law thus gives us only temporary residence permits to the land we own today. Let's not get too possessive...

The reader is asked to consider the flat, bungalow or any plot of land that he stays in. Go to the land records department in your area and take a title search of the land. A title search basically means a listing of previous owners. Assuming the history is available and goes back far enough in time, here's what you'll most likely find. Say you're living in a high rise. Well, that's because of the 'development' that took place that of construction of that high rise. What was there before? Most likely, a lesser storey house whose owners went in for said development. Go further back... Before that 2-3 storey house existed, maybe there was a single storey bungalow. Go even further back and most likely you'll find it to be just open farmland with a shed like structure in which the farmer stayed. Now imagine, like you, everybody took the same negative and unyielding stand on development. Imagine if all the farmers past and present took this stand. There would be nothing but farmland; no developed plots, no bungalows, no 2 - 3 storey buildings, no high rises, no offices, no IT parks, no factories, no roads, railways, airports; essentially nothing but farmland. In essence, we would be transported thousands of years back in our history to the pre-civilization era. What we call a civilized life with modern apartments, roads, railways, airports, offices, factories manufacturing the goods we need, even say hospitals, educational institutes, to our government offices, legislatures, courts etc. everything that we see standing made of brick and mortar today is because some farmer in yesteryear decided to part with his farmland and start the process that has yielded the modern civilization that we see around us.

Getting religion back into the debate and with apologies for the same, to me, those who come in the way of development are committing the gravest of sins. They are condemning themselves, their children and all future generations to a life of stagnation. Although on shorter time scales the pernicious effects of retarded development may not seem obvious, over many years, decades and centuries, the effect of development or rather the lack of thereof will become apparent. For e.g. it would be hard to deny that the quality of our lives today is significantly superior to that of our remote ancestors. Lack of development stagnates growth... That wheel of time that I so vividly remember seeing as a child in the serial 'Mahabharat' (Indian soap) [14] with the voice in the background saying 'main samay hoon' (I am time) always moving, always marching from the past to the future will grind to a halt...

6. No peace without development...

In the words of UN Secretary-General Ban Ki-moon "*There can be no peace without development... no development without peace...*" [15].

As has been oft said about India, we have our rights but where are the basic necessities, where is the food? I'm hungry... Economic development goes hand-in-hand with political and intellectual development. We may have a wonderful Democratic Constitution, a respect for basic human rights and a free society to live in, but at the end of the day if we remain poor due to lack of development, do these higher values and rights really matter? A society wherein a large part of its population has to struggle to put food on the table, has millions upon millions of poor, is a society in trouble... Only rights and freedoms do not guarantee peace. A full stomach is an essential ingredient for it... Recall that episode of the French revolution wherein the poor and harangued people of France went up to their queen, Marie Antoinette, and demanded bread and she supposedly retorted that they have cake instead. Talk about adding insult to injury... Now we all know what happened, don't we? Well, the French revolution happened and specifically for her, it was her head being chopped by a guillotine...

If everyone says a 'No' to development, I state that today you may very well live happily in your bungalow but by the time of your children and your grandchildren, there will be a stagnation which sets in. You may well find them abandoning your cherished house and standing outside the US Embassy in long queues hoping for that prized Visa...

As a side note, I make the following statement. Although I do not have empirical evidence to support my hypothesis, I do believe my statement to be true. Further, even if my hypothesis is unfounded, it does not affect the overall conclusions drawn... So here I go... Those who are the most vociferous opponents of voluntarily surrendering land, if adequately compensated, for development and the greater good of the country are the same people who admire the high development levels achieved by other countries notably the US, China etc. and constantly complain as to why our country cannot do the same... Wonder why...

7. Socialist... Capitalist...

Err, I am a socialist... err, no I am a capitalist... err, no...

In this section I take a slightly humorous note on what is otherwise a rather serious topic. I have seen time and again that those who are most possessive about land are of a socialist bent of mind. Now this is just my personal observation... Of course, I could be wrong and of course I have not conducted any such survey and further am quite unaware of any study that actually says this. So well, I could be wrong but again if I am it does not affect the overall conclusions drawn.

Do this experiment with anyone in your family, friends etc. Ask them their opinion on the Govt. acquiring land say for some public infrastructure project. Whatever the answer, next ask them about their political / economic beliefs. Basically do they subscribe to the capitalist or the socialist way of thinking? Most likely and this is a conjecture only, if the answer is 'No' to the first query meaning they are against any forcible acquisition, to the second query the answer will more likely than not be that the said person is a socialist. The response would be somewhat like yes I believe in socialism, I am a socialist... I abhor the capitalist system of conspicuous consumption, I believe in being thrifty, our founding fathers like Nehru, Gandhi were also socialists and so on...

Now, I am not going to start a fresh debate between socialism and capitalism, although to me the better system is obvious, but herein lies the rub... One of the most basic principles of socialism is State ownership of assets. Assets belong not to the individual but to the state including and most importantly; land. The state has absolute right to take away said land and relocate you somewhere else, to use your land for public infrastructure projects etc. The state or its sub branch known as a collective owns your asset. I repeat, they have the absolute power to take away and reallocate the asset to whosoever they deem fit or forfeit it for public use for the overall benefit of the state. Since most of those countries following the socialist model with regards economic interests also follow the communist system with regards political rule, you would be wise to comply with any such directive. Failure could result in the death penalty or deportation to a concentration camp wherein exist the most sub human conditions imaginable from which you would be lucky to come out alive...

I repeat, under socialism land is a state asset and individual ownership is outlawed. The concept of land belonging to the individual and not the state is a very capitalist idea. So to all my socialist friends who feel entitled to land, I say this; your belief system is a paradox in itself...

Now, let us get to the practical reality facing us in India. Given our exploding population, we have to convert one storey bungalows into multi storey apartments and further into taller skyscrapers. How else are we planning to house everyone? Those who are living in a bungalow are living in luxury while the hundred odd people who could have otherwise been housed in a multi storied apartment on that same place have now to seek out a place far away, face the daily hellish commute to work or in extreme cases just eke out a living staying on the footpath. These are some social issues for the socialists amongst you to consider.

Thus, I proclaim that let us all take a more unselfish view with the aim being the benefit of all...

8. Role of Government...

Till this stage, I have been exhorting the reader to consider the overall good of society. Difficult, I agree, though not impossible... However, there are many steps the government can also take to make this difficult path, less so and mitigate to a large extent any ensuing distress caused.

8.1. Due compensation to be provided

This one is a no brainer... The property owner must be duly compensated for his property. The compensation should be fair and at current market rates. Anything less and the whole scheme will fall apart. In fact, the Act of 2013 [2] proposes remuneration which is up to four times the market value in rural areas and twice the market value in urban areas [16]. To me, if implemented correctly, this is quite sufficient. Many in the media and in politics opposed to this Bill proclaim it to be short changing the farmer. Not so... Let us all take the time to read the Bill and make an informed judgment on its merits / demerits and avoid the risk of getting swayed by political half-truths and grandstanding on issues.

The law does indeed provide for due compensation, in fact more than due compensation. Again, some would complain that corruption eats away at this amount. Possible, I will not deny that corruption exists in our country but I do give a few suggestions below to mitigate its major effects...

8.2. Do away with Capital Gains Tax and Stamp Duty on Property

Even when the government is ready to pay in-between 200% to 400% of the 'market value', this may still fall short of the true market value of land. Surprised and confused; let me explain... Market value of land is 'officially' determined by referring to what are called the Ready Reckoner rates. These rates are compiled by the government by analyzing Sale deeds over some fixed time period, say over the past year in that area. From analyzing these multiple Sale deeds, one can determine the average rate at which land is being bought / sold. These rates are then tabulated in a book called the Ready Reckoner. Sounds reasonable and a correct way to go about market discovery... Yes, but the problem is such; what monetary figure is put in the Sale deed by the buyer / seller is in most cases much less than what the actual deal took place at. This difference is settled the black market way i.e. in cash. The main reasons for this are to reduce the Stamp Duty (which is a percentage of Sale value) and also pay a lower Capital Gains Tax. The higher the amount the seller enters in the Sale deed, the higher the difference will be from his purchase and sale price and thus higher the capitals gains tax that will be payable. Similarly the higher the price as quoted in the Sale deed, the higher the Stamp Duty.

Thus when the government uses these artificially reduced figures based on the Ready Reckoner to calculate the worth of land, it results in gross under reporting of the actual price. So any remuneration given to the farmer based on these low rates will be below par...

I will quote from my personal experience. I and a group of friends, wanted to buy land on the outskirts of Lonavala (a hill station close to Mumbai). Now, the seller (whom I will obviously not name) quoted me around one crore (10 million) for the land but he wanted on the official Sale deed an amount of only twenty lakh rupees (2 million). The rest eighty lakhs (8 million) I was required to pay him by cash. Now obviously the deal did not go through as I did not accept his terms. Now, his logic of course being that the lesser the amount that is shown in the sale deed, the lesser capital gains tax he will have to pay and the lesser amount of Stamp Duty I will have to pay. So according to him it was a win-win.

In short, what is happening is that these taxes are encouraging a thriving black market in our country which not only reduces the amount of tax actually collected, thus prima facie defeating the very purpose for which these taxes were levied in the first place, but more relevant to our present discussion, artificially reduces and fudges land rates. For e.g. if the above Sale deed was executed, the Ready Reckoner rates for that area would have shown an artificially low rate of twenty lakhs rather than the true value of one crore. Now, if the government were to acquire adjacent land and even pay 400% compensation i.e. eighty lakhs based on this Ready Reckoner value, it still is short of the actual rate going on in that area. Thus even if more than adequate compensation is offered, it may still fall short of the actual land value as these land values are calculated on misrepresented information.

As a side note, these taxes are encouraging a booming black market to such an extent that in my opinion, land dealings represent the biggest source of black money in our country. I don't have figures to justify my claim, but I repeat; to me the biggest source of black money is agricultural land dealings and not cash stashed away in Swiss bank accounts. The Swiss money we cannot get back unless the Swiss co-operate. This black money, we can stop by eliminating these taxes, something lying entirely within our jurisdiction.

Thus I propose to do away both these taxes altogether. This way, people are not wary of mentioning the true value of land in their Sale deeds which will then go a long way in market discovery of the true prevailing rates and will then make any compensation awarded commensurate with the value of the land so acquired.

To those who will obviously complain of decline in tax revenues, my rejoinder is as follows... Due to these taxes, the true value in most land transactions is badly fudged and the tax payable is therefore reduced to a bare minimum in most cases. Further, the seller in many cases just avoids paying any Capital Gains tax. Tax avoidance being systemic in our country... Thus for a small accrual resulting from these taxes, we are inviting a lot of heart burn. Capital Gains tax represents a small percentage of the total tax collected by the government. Let us do away with it... Aren't we already doing the same in Equities? Stocks held for more than one year are Capital Gains exempt and there is no significant Stamp Duty on buying and selling stocks. Thus, I cannot overstate this more... Doing away with these pernicious taxes in land transactions will go a long way in establishing a true and efficient land market wherein land becomes more of a commodity, will make the process of acquisition easier and compensation fairer and has the added advantage of destroying to a large extent the black market economy of our country. A win-win for all...

8.3. Land; a Central Subject

Let the Centre get more involved in the planning of cities, towns and villages... Land, although on the concurrent list in our Constitution [17], is mainly treated as a state subject with each state having its own laws relating to buying and selling of land, levy of state taxes like stamp duty etc. Further, each state legislates its own Rent Act, which to me are the most convoluted and lopsided pieces of legislation ever drafted, although that is a topic for another day... Going even further each sub unit of the State like the local Zilla Parishad or Municipal Corporation has its own DP (Development Plan) rules each similar to each other but also subtlety different. To master them all is neigh impossible. To me, this is bizarre... We need uniformity in planning and uniformity in laws to unlock the huge untapped potential of land and its development in our country.

For e.g. I will not buy land in Gujarat as the documents are in Gujarati, the land records are in Gujarati, the land laws of Gujarat are alien to me, especially the Rent laws and so on. I know a bit about Maharashtra and I will stick to it. If however, we have one law governing the whole country and one system, it will allow for people across states an opportunity to try taking the plunge, opening up new buyers for our land owners, chiefly farmers wherein many of these same people are too afraid or wary to take the plunge today.

Therefore, let's take away land planning from the officers and bureaucrats sitting in some Zilla Parishad, Corporation or even at the State level. Incorporate one Central planning committee, hire the best talent and draft laws universally applicable across our land. Involve even foreign architects, design firms, planners etc. For e.g. in Dubai all the planning is centralized and all the best talent from across the world gets to design their buildings. What an effect it has had... Build new cities from scratch... Rather than going by one building redevelopment after another which is a terribly inefficient as it does not solve infrastructure problems like road bottlenecks, water scarcity etc. Like China go in for planned cities from the ground up having the best infrastructure facilities provided from scratch. For that we have to do away with local arcane laws. As an aside, the recent development plan issued by the BMC was so full of errors that it had to be scrapped [18]. Incompetence or corruption, I don't know and I don't want to know. There is a better way, that's all I will say... Thus let's introduce Legislation to this effect; let's make Land a Central subject.

Further, go in for Computerization of land records including using GPS to determine and map accurate boundaries, calculate areas etc. Have one database for the entire country rather than individual Taluka's having their records which are anyways shabbily maintained with the data not being updated and in many cases reflecting the names of previous owners or those who are long since deceased... Making land, not a local subject, a state subject but rather a central subject with a central monitoring institute to plan cities, development of villages using latest computer technology, satellite information of the terrain, population distribution etc., say a bit of how China approaches its development or how Dubai is doing it... The way going forward is to involve world renowned architects, design firms, construction companies to get the job done. For e.g., the Mumbai Pune expressway partly was built by a Malaysian firm [3]. No problem... As long as a good job is done, who did it is immaterial. One more idea would be to link the land records to the Aadhaar card so that seamless money transfers are made directly to the people whose land has been acquired. This avoids government middle men from entering into the picture...

In essence I proclaim; one country; one land; one law...

8.4. Mobile fast track courts

Even when duly compensated and even when given up to two to four times the compensation [16], there can still be disagreements with regards the fair value of the land, the rights of heirs (if the original owner is no more) etc. Some litigation is any large project is to be expected... For the aggrieved parties to go through the regular Court process would be a slow and expensive process. Further, if any one party were to get a 'stay order', the entire project can get inordinately delayed leading to massive time and cost overruns. To avoid many of the disadvantages of long drawn out litigation, I suggest establishing in the new Land Amendment Bill [1] fast track courts similar to tribunals that specifically deal only with this issue. Further that they be set-up near the acquisition site so as to be easily approachable. Let's call them mobile fast track courts... Let them dispense with speedy and efficient justice... In fact, a few clauses of the Civil Procedure Code could also be relaxed. According to me in the majority of cases people having some grievances will readily accept their judgments. Of course for aggrieved parties further appeal can always be done to the next higher court in the 'regular' judiciary. In this way, I believe, the vast majority of litigation can be settled in a timely manner wherein the affected parties feel satisfied that a hearing at some judicial level was indeed given to them.

9. The Threat from China...

The reader must be wondering whether I have lost track of the topic at hand. What has China got anything to do with land? At first glance, probably nothing... However the remainder of this book will be exclusively used to convince the reader that it does and it does so with such importance and urgency so as to make all the previously enumerated points, even though relevant, sound mute in comparison... So let me start... First I spell out the threat posed by China. This should be of grave concern to us in its own right, irrespective of its relevance to this particular topic.

In this new world order being created, it can hardly be denied that China is emerging as the new superpower. It has probably the strongest and most robust economy of date. With money, comes political influence, military might and the ability to reshape the rest of the world to its way... The era in which the Unites States held this mantle of leadership for many years especially from the end of the Second World War is now on the wane with its struggling economy, mortgage crisis, aging population and a huge debt pegged at some eighteen trillion dollars [19]. Further, this is compounded by a gross inability to grow as it has reached significant levels of development already.

The Chinese economy on the other hand has a huge trade surplus, has astronomical levels of foreign exchange reserves, is growing at a fairly rapid pace and should by many estimates, say by around 2021 [20] overtake that of the US to become the world's largest. One of the big advantages the Chinese have over the US is its huge population... Even if I were to assume that an average Chinese earns half of that of the average American (currently it is much less) even then the total Chinese economy by virtue of its vastly greater population (China has 1.371 billion while the US has 321 million [21]) would be more than twice the size of the US economy.

Now, the million dollar question is who can counter an economy of 1.371 billion consumers? Well the answer is simple; an economy having 1.276 billion [21] consumers, or in other words, India... So going forward, the only nation that can (and I am not saying will) challenge Chinese supremacy in the world will be India... Now whether India can mount any serious competition to China, only time will tell. However you can be dead sure that the Chinese have definitely factored this into their equation...

What equation am I talking about? It is the unstated and tacit aim of being the most powerful and dominant nation on Earth. This grand plan suffers from just one glitch, a rising, powerful and a developed India...

It is very much ingrained in the Chinese psyche that going forwards it will not be the US but rather India that could emerge as its sole challenger. Thus, it is imperative by them that come what may, India has to be contained... Now, to achieve this goal of 'containing' India, China is using all means possible, both overt and covert to isolate us economically, politically, militarily etc. To many this may sound like I'm making sensationalist claims... However, I submit my evidence as such...

10. I submit evidence to a candid audience

China is very friendly with Pakistan [22]... In fact in a recent visit to Pakistan, the Chinese premier Xi Jinping referred to Pakistan as an 'Asian Tiger' [23]. Now, what I wonder do these two nations have in common? One is an emerging industrial and economic power, the other's economy is tethering on the brink. One is a State that does not believe in religion, the other is Islamic Fundamentalist. China is itself very much concerned with terrorism in its Muslim majority Xinjiang province [24]. On the other hand, Pakistan is a State sponsorer of terrorism [25]. On a lighter side, in one nation the meat Pork is eaten regularly, it being a national dish of sorts and in the other it is considered to be the most 'haram' and even possession of it can land you in jail or worse. In short nothing, except that they share a common adversary; India. The saying goes that an enemy's enemy is my friend.

I proceed below to enumerate a select list of references detailing the threat we face from an ascendant China. I could fill pages upon pages on this but that would be straying a bit. Of course, there are many sources online and in print wherein similar information is available. The interested reader can find a plethora of information on this topic.

10.1. Pakistan's Nuclear Bomb

In violation of the Nuclear Non-Proliferation treaty China helped Pakistan develop the nuclear bomb [26] [27] [28] [29] [30]. Thus, one of the biggest threats to our very existence can be attributed to China...

Excerpts from a book interview in the US News by former U.S. Air Force Secretary Thomas Reed [26]

Why, as you say in the book, did the Chinese give the technology to Pakistan?

Pakistan can be explained by a balance of power: India was China's enemy and Pakistan was India's enemy. The Chinese did a massive training of Pakistani scientists, brought them to China for lectures, even gave them the design of the CHIC-4 device, which was a weapon that was easy to build a model for export. There is evidence that A.Q. Khan used Chinese designs in his nuclear designs. Notes from those lectures later turned up in Libya, for instance. And the Chinese did similar things for the Saudis, North Koreans, and the Algerians.

Did the Chinese further assist in the Pakistani program?

Under Pakistani president Benazir Bhutto, the country built its first functioning nuclear weapon. We believe that during Bhutto's term in office, the People's Republic of China tested Pakistan's first bomb for her in 1990. There are numerous reasons why we believe this to be true, including the design of the weapon and information gathered from discussions with Chinese nuclear experts. That's why the Pakistanis were so quick to respond to the Indian nuclear tests in 1998. It only took them two weeks and three days. When the Soviet Union took the United States by surprise with a test in 1961, it took the U.S. seventeen days to prepare and test, a device that had been on hand for years. The Pakistani response makes it clear that the gadget tested in May 1998 was a carefully engineered device in which they had great confidence.

End excerpts...

Excerpts from China, Pakistan, and the Bomb: The Declassified File on U.S. Policy, 1977-1997; National Security Archive Electronic Briefing Book No. 114 [27]

China's professed opposition to sharing nuclear weapons technology with non-nuclear states may have led to compromise of principle when security and economic interests were at stake. Well before the question of nuclear sharing emerged, China and Pakistan, each having an adversarial relationship with India, had developed a close understanding involving significant military cooperation. When the U.S. cut off sales of weapons to both India and Pakistan because of their 1965 border conflict, China became Pakistan's main supplier of weapons. The close relationship with China became one of the pillars of Pakistani foreign policy. When India held its first nuclear test in 1974, and Pakistan made decisions to acquire its own capability to build nuclear weapons, it may have seemed a matter of course for elements in the Chinese military, which had a powerful voice in Beijing's nuclear establishment, eventually to decide to lend Pakistan a hand.

End excerpts...

Excerpts from the Huffington Post [28]

Pakistan's nuclear arsenal and superior delivery system has in a real sense neutralized India's overwhelming advantage in conventional military terms that it enjoyed over Pakistan. By building up Pakistan's nuclear arsenal and missile systems, China has effectively checkmated India and blind-sided its challenge as China's main Asian rival.

End excerpts...

Excerpts from the Wall Street Journal [29]

Even China is now raising flags about nuclear proliferation. Beijing helped Pakistan get the bomb in the 1980's and has been North Korea's patron from one Dear Leader to the next. But in February Chinese officials warned a group of Americans that Pyongyang has many more nuclear warheads than previously believed: up to 20 already, perhaps 40 by next year.

End excerpts...

Excerpts from the New York Times [30]

China, a staunch ally of Pakistan's, provided blueprints for the bomb, as well as highly enriched uranium, tritium, scientists and key components for a nuclear weapons production complex, among other crucial tools. Without China's help, Pakistan's bomb would not exist, said Gary Milhollin, a leading expert on the spread of nuclear weapons.

End excerpts...

To me, nothing would please China more than if India and Pakistan, now two nuclear powers (Pakistan's arsenal, courtesy the Chinese) wage war and end up destroying one another.

In the words of the Chinese philosopher San Tzu *"The art of war is to win one without fighting"*.

10.2. Pakistan says "I have the Bomb; thank you China... But how do I deliver it to India..."

China again to the rescue... To deliver a nuclear warhead, the best way is to mount it on a ballistic missile and launch it towards your enemy. Most of Pakistan's missiles like the Nasr, Ghauri, Shaheen etc. are Chinese rip-offs [31] [32] [33] [34]. So again we have the Chinese to 'thank' for arming our neighbor. Needless to mention that all of these technology transfers done by the Chinese are in violation of the Missile Technology Control Regime but no one in the world has the nerve to bring China to book...

Excerpts from the Wikipedia article on Nasr (missile) [31]

The Hatf IX Nasr is a ballistic missile which carries a sub-kiloton nuclear warhead out to a range of 60 km (37.3 mi). It is believed to be derived from the WS-2 Weishi Rockets system developed by China's Sichuan Aerospace Corporation. Four missiles are carried on the same Chinese-origin 8x8 transporter erector launcher (TEL) as the Pakistan Army's A-100E 300mm Multiple Launch Rocket System (MLRS), a Chinese version of the BM-30 Smerch.

End excerpts...

Excerpts from the International Assessment and Strategy Center [32]

Pakistan's capability to build small plutonium warheads is widely reported to have developed thanks to the assistance of the PRC. China is very likely the source for a range of non-nuclear warheads for the Shaheen 2, Shaheen 1 and Ghaznavi missiles. For its DF-11 Mod 1 SRBM, China is reported to have developed high-explosive cluster warheads, which use a large number of small warheads for attacking soft targets, and thermobaric warheads, which destroy by producing fantastic heat and pressure. And according to a U.S. source, Pakistan is a suspected recipient for new Chinese radio-frequency (RF) missile warheads. These can produce a large electromagnetic pulse via a conventional explosion and are used to attack electronic infrastructure.

Shaheen 2. Pakistan's largest and most capable ballistic missile is the two-stage Shaheen 2, or Hatf 6, reported by the U.S. intelligence community to have been developed with China's assistance. To date, this missile has no publicly identified counterpart in the Chinese missile arsenal, but one possibility might be the DF-25, a reported two-stage 1,700-2,500km range solid-fuel missile.

Shaheen 1. First revealed in 1999, the Shaheen 1, or Hatf 4, also has no known Chinese equivalent, but its Chinese origins are more apparent than the Shaheen 2. The nose section is very clearly a copy of that seen on the Chinese DF-11 Mod 1 missile first revealed in their October 1999 military parade.

Ghaznavi. The latest Pakistani missile is the Ghaznavi, or Hatf 3, which was formally adopted by the Strategic Forces Command on February 22, 2004. This appears to be an exact copy of the latest version of the DF-11 Mod 1

End excerpts...

Excerpts from www.indiandefensenews.in [33]

In the mid 1990's China supplied around 30 knocked down M-11 missiles to Pakistan, which also included launch platforms. It is reported that more than 80 M-11 missiles were delivered. It is also widely acknowledged that China provided the blueprints for a 1966 design of a U-235 nuclear-implosion device. This missile warhead was reported to weigh about 1,300 kilograms with a yield of up to 25 kilotons.

On 15 April 1999 Pakistan tested the Shaheen thus confirming Pakistan's missile imports from China. The claimed 750 km range of the Shaheen of is roughly double the standard range of the M-11, and is consistent with the range of the much large

Chinese M-9. However, images and videos however suggested that tested "Shaheen" missile was clearly the M-9, not the M-11, and the Shaheen Transporter Erector Launcher [TEL] was ostensibly a modified version of the Chinese M-11 TEL.

The Shaheen-1 missile is China's M-9 missile, which Islamabad acquired in 1991 but had kept under wraps for fear of sanctions. Pakistan is believed to have a capability to deploy a nuclear warhead weighing around 500 kilograms. If its ascribed range/payload curve proves out, the Hatf-4 / Shaheen would have sufficient range from relatively secure positions west of the border with India.

End excerpts...

10.3. China's game to checkmate India...

China is also actively pursuing other military and non-military avenues like economic co-operation, political support to our neighbors, giving aid etc. to cement its relationship with countries in our backyard. Thus they are trying to marginalize our influence in our own neighborhood. Sometimes they have been successful, sometimes not, but try they will... There is also a plethora of information on this topic and I'm sure the reader would have already come across some newspaper article, online resource etc. highlighting Chinese expansionist claims in the Indian Ocean region. I detail a few resources below:

Excerpts from the Jamestown Foundation [35]

The second leg of the Chinese strategy to prevail over India is directed at gaining military linkages and economic influence amongst India's South Asian neighbors.

Burma, which was recognized by both the British and the Japanese as "the back door to India," has in the past three decades been targeted by China to steadily increase its political, military and economic influence. It bought its way into favor with the Myanamarese Burmese military government by facilitating a peace agreement with the Communist Party of Burma, selling them nearly US$ 2 billion of arms, providing cheap consumer goods, re-building strategic surface communications and upgrading port facilities to enhance maritime activities. This strategy has given it considerable strategic leverage including a secure hinterland to the Indian Ocean from where it can prosecute its seaward strategy.

China remains--overwhelmingly--the main supplier of arms to Sri Lanka, which lies off the southern tip of India, and provides military equipment and materials to Bangladesh as well.

The pincer movement to isolate India from other South Asian militaries is completed by the massive arms supplies to Pakistan and assistance of technological, material and human resources to enhance its fledgling defense industrial establishment.

A fourth and equally ominous leg of China's strategy to gain leverage over India lies in its national water resource strategy. One of the objects of which is to manipulate the Asian sources of water to establish a 'hands off' control over the river basins flowing through other regional powers that China considers a threat to its long term national interests. This strategy will hold millions of Indians hostage to Chinese potential to flood them or withhold their water supply.

End excerpts...

Excerpts from the Wikipedia article on String of Pearls (Indian Ocean) [36]

The String of Pearls theory is a geopolitical theory regarding potential Chinese intentions in the Indian Ocean region. It refers to the network of Chinese military and commercial facilities and relationships along its sea lines of communication, which extend from the Chinese mainland to Port Sudan. The sea lines run through several major maritime choke points such as the Strait of Mandeb, the Strait of Malacca, the Strait of Hormuz and the Lombok Strait, as well as other strategic maritime centers in Pakistan, Sri Lanka, Bangladesh, the Maldives and Somalia.

For years, China has sought to encircle South Asia with a "string of pearls": A network of ports connecting its eastern coast to the Middle East that would boost its strategic clout and maritime access. Not surprisingly, India as well as other countries have regarded this process with serious concern. For example, China concluded a multibillion-dollar deal with Pakistan in order to develop the port at Gwadar, owing to its strategic location at the mouth of the Strait of Hormuz, which more than offsets the port's limited commercial potential.

Twice last autumn, Chinese attack submarines docked at Sri Lanka's newly opened, $500 million container terminal at Colombo Harbor. The harbor has been built and is majority-owned by Chinese state companies. China has now embarked on a $1.4-billion project to build a sprawling complex roughly the size of Monaco on reclaimed land in Colombo – a "port city" that will become a major stop on China's nautical "road."

End excerpts...

Excerpts from www.firstpost.com [37]

The latest manifestation is the Chinese initiative in Pakistan linking Kashgar in Chinese held Sinkiang to Gwadar in Balochistan, via Pakistani Occupied Kashmir and Gilgit - Baltistan. The proposed $46 billion project has a number of alarming and sinister implications, almost none of which is good for India.

The simplest first: in the Chinese maps that have been reprinted by many in the global media, Chinese-Occupied Kashmir (CoK, or Aksai Chin) is not even marked as disputed territory: it has been integrated into Chinese Sinkiang. Interestingly, western media that insists on drawing dotted lines around all of Kashmir and marking it ostentatiously as a disputed territory has quietly accepted this. Score 1 to the usual Chinese tactic of "creating facts on the ground", as they did with suddenly referring to the Senkaku Islands with a new name, Daiyou, now widely accepted as an alternative.

More alarmingly, the Chinese are proposing building roads, pipelines, and suchlike projects through Gilgit - Baltistan (GB) and Pakistan - Occupied Kashmir (PoK), which India considers its sovereign territory. It is a serious offense in India to publish any map that does not show the entirety of Jammu and Kashmir as part of India. The blatant violation of Indian sentiment and of its long-stated diplomatic stance that GB/PoK are forbidden territories are a direct challenge to India. It is also intended to put India on the defensive when PM Narendra Modi visits China as scheduled this month. The Pakistan deal will be presented to PM

Modi as a fait accompli, a non-negotiable fact on the ground, much like China invaded Vietnam during Vajpayee's 1979 visit to Beijing: a 'loss of face', a snub.

End excerpts...

As Zhou Bo, an honorary fellow with the Chinese People's Liberation Army Academy of Military Science admits that China's mega-projects *"will fundamentally change the political and economic landscape of the Indian Ocean"* [38]...

11. My myopic foresight...

The only way India can counter the growing Chinese threat is by itself growing fast and keeping pace with Chinese levels of development. There is a great asymmetry in our achievements compared to that of the Chinese and it's only growing with each passing day.

I keep repeating this; high levels of development can only be achieved by building roads, railways, factories, establishing new companies, investing in R and D, innovating, inventing new technologies, setting-up world class educational facilities and so on. We will have to build new cities that contribute to economic growth and at the same time decongest old cities which would involve large scale shifting of populations. Now, to do all of this would require as a starting point a change in mindset. A readiness to surrender land for the greater public good...

If we don't do this, the asymmetry between our two nations will only get worse with the result being an emboldened China. With the US economy in decline and with us lagging so far behind, there may well come a time when the Chinese elite decide it's time to 'finish' India. A lightening war with us... The

Germans called it Blitzkrieg when they rolled into France. The US called it Shock and Awe in Iraq.

This asymmetry in our levels of development has a direct one-on-one correspondence with asymmetry in military might. The Chinese economy is stronger, bigger and along with their massive manufacturing capability can not only mass produce, i-Phones but can only mass produce tanks, aircraft, battleships etc. Their military is bigger and better equipped than ours with their yearly budget being 216 billion dollars [39] compared to ours which is 50 billion dollars [39].

The reader may well call me a 'cry wolf', and thus the title of this section. I may well have a one track mindset, a myopic point of view and you may well not agree with my 'war mongering' outlook. Maybe you're right but here's the million dollar question, what if I am? Can we afford to take this risk? We have already fought one war before, haven't we, and we are all aware of what their false promises of peace of 'Hindi Chini Bhai Bhai' actually meant...

Thus, it is now time we declared in our minds, actions, deeds and in all aspects other than political a 'State of Emergency'. A crash program of building infrastructure, industries and so on... To me, it is abundantly clear; we are fighting for our very survival itself...

Our slow pace of growth vis-à-vis the Chinese so often compared to that of the hare and tortoise has a sad ending for us. Yes, in the fable, the tortoise does win but that's only because the hare takes an unscheduled break. No sign the Chinese will do that... Further, do note that this is not a contest in which, once over, the winner and loser sportingly shake hands and walk away...

I say to thee that because you did not give up your land, because therefore, for e.g., some factory for manufacturing iron and steel could not be set up, because therefore some iron bullet could not be made, because therefore some Indian army officers gun ran out of ammunition, because therefore he was shot dead by his Chinese counterpart having an immense supply of said bullets due to his country's immense manufacturing capability. Do our soldiers risk less? Do we want their life on our soul? Hail the sacrifice that our brave soldiers make... Is it not that their sacrifice is greater than ours; we only have to part with our land not our life... Further, can giving up our land when duly compensated even be called a sacrifice?

For those who say industrial might does not matter, what only matters is the bravery of our soldiers. No... Science and technology have progressed so far and so beyond human endurance that we just cannot compare. For e.g. even two hundred years ago, using rather primitive technology by our modern standards, a small nation that you'll be hard pressed to point on a world map ruled most of the world. I, of course, refer to Great Britain. Why? It's because of scientific progress and industrial might... It may sound lame but it beats bravery every time...

12. Old Chinese saying...

'If you want to be rich, first build roads' [40]... I jot down some of the mega projects undertaken by the Chinese. Most readers would surely have heard of the big ticket infrastructure developments done in China and I could myself fill pages upon pages detailing them but that would be straying a bit. Therefore, I stick to this one reference. Of course, there are many other sources online wherein similar data is available. The interested reader can find a plethora of information on this topic.

Excerpts from blog.sina.com.cn [41]

- Changxing Island shipbuilding base; creating the world's largest shipbuilding base (35 billion yuan)

- The Beijing-Shanghai high-speed railway; the world's longest high-speed rail project (220 billion yuan)

- Beijing South railway station; Asia's largest railway station (6.3 billion yuan)

- The world's longest Cross-Sea Bridge of Hangzhou Bay (16 billion yuan)

- Su-Tong Yangtze River cable-stayed bridge; the world's largest (7.89 billion yuan)

- Five vertical and seven horizontal National Highway trunk lines (900 billion yuan)

- China's eight horizontal and eight vertical large-capacity optical fiber communication network (7 billion yuan)

- The T3 terminal of Beijing Capital International Airport; the world's largest single building projects (25 billion yuan)

- Donghai island of Zhanjiang: millions of tons of iron and steel (69 billion yuan)

- Shanghai Lingang new town; the world's largest reclamation project (150 billion yuan)

- The Yangshan deep water port; creating the world's largest port (50 billion yuan)

- Sichuan-East natural gas transmission project (62.7 billion yuan)

- Liaoning Hongyanhe nuclear power plant (50 billion yuan)

- Strategic petroleum reserve project (100 billion yuan)

- Kunming new airport International Airport – China's 4th largest aviation hub (23.1 billion yuan)

- Hainan power grid across the sea (2.2 billion yuan)

- Tianjin million ton ethylene project (26.8 billion yuan)

- Shanghai light laboratory; China's major scientific projects (1.2 billion yuan)

- The revival of the Silk Road program (43 billion US$)

- China's second largest hydropower station at Xiluodu hydropower station (79.2 billion yuan)

- Hainan Wenchang space launch site (12 billion yuan)

- The large plane project in Shanghai (30.05 trillion yuan)

- The Spallation Neutron Source project (1.2 billion yuan)

- The world's largest 500 meter aperture spherical radio telescope (627 million yuan)

- The Shanghai-Chengdu Expressway (170 billion yuan)

- Ningxia Ningdong energy and chemical industry base (100 billion yuan)

- The Hong Kong-Zhuhai-Macao Bridge (70 billion yuan)

- Jiuquan, Gansu province--the world's largest wind power base (120 billion yuan)

- The national plan of civil airport distribution (450 billion yuan)

- Shanghai HongQiao transportation hub (36 billion yuan)

- Tianjin offshore drilling (22 billion yuan)

- Energy and chemical industry base in northern Shaanxi (90 billion yuan)

- Sinopec Iran Yadavaran Field (2 billion US$)

- Petro China's Sudanese oil project (7 billion US$)

- CNPC Niger oil project (5 billion US$)

- Beilin added iron in Gabon in Africa (2.7 billion US$)

- Eleven-Five national grid construction (1.215 trillion yuan)

- China's investment in Nigeria's railway modernization project (8.3 billion US$)

- China's investment in Libya a coastal railway line project (2.6 billion US$)

- Russia Baltic Pearl project (1.3 billion US$)

- China's investment in Algeria-west highway projects (7 billion US$)

- Qinzhou, Guangxi million-ton oil refining project (15.2 billion yuan)

- Shanghai Tower; the tallest building in China (7 billion yuan)

- Xuanhan, Sichuan giant gas field (70 billion yuan)

- The 2010 Shanghai World Expo (40 billion yuan)

- Southern Salon sink shipbuilding base (4.5 billion yuan)

- Zhejiang Sanmen nuclear power project (80 billion yuan)

- Guangdong Yangjiang nuclear power station (8 billion US$)

- Yantai, Shandong Haiyang nuclear power station (60 billion yuan)

- 80,000 tons of multi-direction forging hydraulic press (1.517 billion yuan)

- Dalian into China's biggest oil refinery base (10.7 billion yuan)

- Chongqi bridge (7.6 billion yuan)

- Chengdu Shuangliu International Airport extension project (12.7 billion yuan)

- The Pearl River Delta inter-city rail transit network (100 billion yuan)

- The Yangtze River Delta inter-city rail transit network (150 billion yuan)

- The Shanghai Yangtze River tunnel and bridge (12.6 billion yuan)

- Anhui Huaibei billion tone coal base (70 billion yuan)

- Billions of pounds of quality rice production project in Jiangxi province (31.8 billion yuan)

- Qinling Zhongnanshan tunnel; the longest highway tunnel in China (2.5 billion yuan)

- 12 great hydropower base in China (2 trillion yuan)

- The Shanghai-Hangzhou Maglev project (22 billion yuan)

- The Shanghai world financial center (7 billion yuan)

- The vegetable basket project (50 billion yuan)

- Tianjin Lingang industrial area (300 billion yuan)

- Wuhan Tianxingzhou Yangtze River Bridge (11 billion yuan)

- 720 million farmers in new cooperative medical service (100 billion yuan)

End excerpts...

Plus countless other medium and small infrastructure projects... Read it and be awed... I give them my standing ovation... Just ask yourselves this question; could any of these have been possible without acquiring land? I think not...

13. We were a British colony... We are now a Chinese colony...

Yes, I know, you'll be protesting this above statement and probably with much vehemence... How dare I make such a claim...? Well, of course, you are right; we are Not a Chinese colony...

However, let's examine this claim for a moment with cooler heads... The way I see it, colonization is a poisonous two headed snake. One aspect of colonization is the political control over the lands being so colonized for e.g. direct rule. Yes, the British did that... We did have their Union Jack flying over us for a hundred plus years. Of course, and I'll agree with you that China does not rule us in that sense or even have much political influence in our country. We do not see the Chinese Five-star Red Flag in lieu of our Tri-color on our lands (except probably Aksai Chin but that's another story).

However, there is a second and much more important aspect of colonization which to me is far more poisonous of those two heads i.e. economic colonization. The British banned factories, industries, skilled labor and any higher development other than agriculture in India. We became only a supplier of cheap raw materials for their industries and a market for their finished goods. Finished goods being worth more in value than the original raw materials led us to an unfavorable balance of trade with them. They ended up getting richer and we, poorer... I state that it is this economic colonization that did the maximum damage. From one of the richest nations of yesteryear, we became one of the poorest...

What about China? Well, the story is eerily similar... Our trade balance is badly skewed in favor of the Chinese. Our exports to China stand at USD 12 billion while we import a whopping USD 60 billion [42]. What is worse, of what we export, a large part is raw materials, for e.g., iron ore to be used by their factories [42]. They then manufacture the finished goods and export them back to us. Check the back label on almost any item in your house; TV, mobile, refrigerator, AC etc. and more likely than not, you'll find 'made in China' imprinted on it...

Drawing on parallels with the British, would it be too much of a stretch of the imagination to claim that we are a Chinese colony now; well at least in the economic sense... So dependent on them that were they to sanction us today, we would find it difficult to carry on a modern lifestyle considering that most of the goods and modern day amenities that we now take for granted, a few which are enumerated above, coming from them...

When the British ruled us we didn't have much of a choice in deciding our economic policies. But today we do... Shouldn't we exercise that choice to enact legislation that allows for us becoming an industrial power rather than a backwater agricultural country? Shouldn't we willingly and happily surrender land for our nation's progress...?

To me it's strange and sad that this is not what is happening... Strange that a Democracy in which the welfare of the people is to be put first, their development is to be put first is rather bowing down to a select special interest group of farmers and landowners. Strange that many people, maybe even a majority of people, both farmers and others alike support this uncompromising stand on land acquisition. Strange, that many of our elected leaders are taking a similar stand... Strange that the net result of all this is that a people's elected government, the people themselves are actively if unknowingly participating in making their own country an economic colony of another... Strange indeed...

14. Is China really better?

I am sure there are many among you who are awed by what the Chinese have achieved. Do count me as one among you'll. It is hard not to be impressed by the tall skyscrapers, fast trains, big wide roads, huge industries, colossal airports, even bigger dams and such. Of course, as I have been constantly saying right through this section on China; this is something we should emulate and strive for. However, although China excels in industry and infrastructure and definitely should be an inspiration in this regard, to my mind, it has nothing else to offer to the world... Let me explain...

Well, firstly and obviously, China has no democracy, no system of universal human rights (what in India we call fundamental rights) like the right to a fair trial, the right of dissent, freedom of speech etc.

How important are these rights vs. say bricks and mortar development and progress has been debated ad nauseam on many chat sites, blogs, TV shows, Internet sites, family debates etc. Conclusions and opinions vary... For me, I will exercise my right to an opinion (incidentally something not very freely available to the Chinese) and I will claim that both are important. Life is somehow incomplete without either...

If industrial development represents progress in the sciences and engineering, a free and fair system of law, upholding of the fundamental rights and the right to choose a Government represents progress in the moral and political sciences... In essence, they represent mankind's intellectual progress through the ages.

Aphorisms like I have a right to disagree with you, to criticize your performance to hold a contra point of view have evolved in our political landscape only recently in the last couple of centuries or so. That everyone is equal and that no one should enjoy special privileges in the law is another example. Further, those who govern should do so only by the consent of the governed sounds innately correct and obvious at a deep level. I strongly believe that all of us are imbibed by a sense of right and wrong and we, given sufficient thought can overcome our personal prejudices and arrive at these very same conclusions.

The Magna Carta, affectionately referred to as the Birth Certificate of Freedom, which started us on this road to freedom and democracy and which states in essence that the King does not enjoy absolute power is a 'development' of the human intellect matching or in my opinion even exceeding the 'development' as represented by bricks and mortar; something that the Chinese currently excel at...

Where am I going with this? Many of us who see the phenomenal development achieved by China feel a sense of despair. Oft mentioned quotes read like; they are just too good, we can never catch up with them etc. I caution against such pessimism... Granted they are exceedingly good in this regard but as I am trying to impress on you, they are far from perfect. For one, they are infinitely far behind us in development of this another sort.

Let me give you a personal example: One uncle of mine, and I will obviously not name him, went on a visit to China. He, like most of us, was overawed by the level of development he saw. On his return we were chatting and he of course was full of praise for the Chinese. Comparing India, USA and China, his conclusions were that USA is now a 'has been' power and China is the new one and of course India stands nowhere in this list. Now, one of the things we have in India which we got from the US and other free societies in the West, well as I have oft repeated by now is freedom of speech. Now, what has this got to do with him, you'll ask in exasperation and I will try answer... Some time back when the Mumbai terrorist attacks happened with Kasab and others going on a shooting spree, this same uncle of mine came to the conclusion that it was all because of our Kashmir dispute with Pakistan. He opined that if the whole of Kashmir were to be handed over to Pakistan, the problem of terrorism will be solved once and for all. Now in my opinion, I am strongly against handing over Kashmir and I also firmly believe that even if this were done, the problem of terrorism will Not get solved. Terrorists can always and will always find alternate supposed grievances on which to take offense and go about their terror business. Anyways, in essence it could be said that me and my uncle have these two opposing points of view... Now, scandalous as his opinion was, my uncle not only put it to me but shared it in a public gathering wherein he indulged in slogan shouting to this effect. Understandably many were upset and he was escorted away from said public place. Now imagine this same uncle of mine, living in China, being a Chinese citizen and saying something similar. For e.g. imagine if he had said something like giving independence to Tibet. Well, if he does say those words in China, God save him... He would have been arrested, probably tortured and even killed. This is how the Chinese Communist system works. As an example, I refer the reader to the case of a Mr. Liu Xiaobo who is a writer and a human rights activist critical of the Chinese one-party Communist rule. The reader may be pleasantly surprised to know that he was awarded the 2010 Nobel Peace Prize for "his long and non-violent struggle for fundamental human rights in China" [43]. Further, as the reader would have guessed, he was unable to attend the ceremony as he was incarcerated in a Chinese prison serving a jail sentence for his 'crimes'. So I say this; my uncle may owe his freedom, probably his very life to the political rights guaranteed by our Constitution which, I would like to remind everyone and him especially, were to a large part borrowed from the ideas as championed in the US (his much reviled nation). My thumbs up to India and the US that he has lived to tell the tale...

So I say this, the world's eyes are on India. In their heart of hearts, they want India to win this battle against China. This is because of the value system that India stands for... It is now up to us to grab this initiative and strive for development. If China wins, I say, it would represent a big step backwards in human intellectual progress. A Communist Dictatorship will win against a Democracy. The hard won freedoms which millions have struggled to achieve through the centuries, from denying the King absolute power to having elected governments, will be lost to history. The sacrifice borne by so many, risking death, imprisonment and torture will come to naught... I with folded hands ask you to consider this; there are surely some things more important than your piece and parcel of land... I repeat; we are the only country that can give China a run for its money. The only country that can stand as an alternate example of how things can be done, both democracy and development combined... If we lose this chance, we'll be doing a great disservice, not only to us but to the whole world and to the exalted ideals for which we and the West stand for... History will judge us very harshly and rightfully so. We let Dictatorship win over Democracy...

15. Am I being paranoid about this...?

Yes, this is the most obvious question to ask. I sometimes wonder the same thing myself. Well, I give my defense as under. I apply, what I call, the 1% rule... There are some things in life that are so important that even a 1% chance of failure or being wrong is not acceptable... Let's take example of flying. If I were to tell you that there is 1% chance of a plane crashing (in reality it's much lower), would you fly? Don't think so... It means that out of every one hundred flights, one will end in disaster. Although the risk is 1%, this is still, too much... I'm sure there may be some of us who have flown more times than that...

Now, the same principle applies here... So, even when what I claim has only a 1% chance, and I personally believe it to be much more, where so much is at stake, we just cannot afford to take the risk...

A thought experiment for the reader... When the first ships of the erstwhile British East India Trading Company landed on our shores, we are told that no Indian ruler of that time could foresee the risk. Let's put ourselves in the shoes of such a ruler. A ship of the East India Company has just made port... It carries a crew of at most a few hundred sailors. Hardly enough to challenge my army of thousands, probably even lakhs. They have come here as traders and are asking permission for commerce. A rather innocuous request, I say... They are carrying small arms and munitions but they are mainly for self protection on voyages across the seas. Their cargo hold is not having any big guns but is rather filled with goods for trade. To the scaremongers in my court who are cautioning me of the danger, I say that I give them a less than 1% chance of ever being able to challenge me, my kingdom, my power base, my huge army etc. etc. etc.

Now we all know what happened don't we...

We berate our rulers for not foreseeing the consequences. Call them dumb, stupid or whatever adjective suits you. Now, I ask, are we any better? I confidently state that we are dumber, stupider and more of whatever adjective you've just used... The reason being that not only do we have a precedent of this happening which they didn't, but I will submit to you that the threat from China is far more obvious, far more 'out in the open' with one battle already fought and China in de facto control of part of what we consider our territory; Aksai Chin. I hope our future generations do not label us as being worse than what we currently label our leaders of yesteryear.

From a mathematical standpoint, human relations which then translate into relations between families, society and nation states are modeled as non linear systems. Now, what does this jargon mean? Well, for most of time, there is an era of peace and tranquility amongst nations. This can last for many years, decades and centuries even. We therefore, take peace for granted. But there could be a growing tension below the surface... We get attuned to a peaceful atmosphere and it becomes part of our habit. We generally do not tend to imagine an era in which peace does not hold. However, there are short periods in which Wars break out which last from a few days, months or at most a few years that usher in catastrophic change. Because we live in peace today, we feel we will live in peace forever... Not so...

To me, China decimating India militarily in some future conflict for which it is actively preparing will be the biggest setback suffered by our nation in its thousands of years of history; bigger than all the wars fought earlier, all the foreign invasions, British rule etc., an existential threat of sorts. I firmly believe that what is at stake is our country, our livelihood, our culture, our very way of life and everything we hold dear...

Thus, I say to thee...

Not giving up land especially when you're compensated and especially when the Chinese threat has been extensively enumerated is a treasonable offense...

16. Conclusion

Coming back to where we originally started from; our discussion was of 'The Right to Fair Compensation and Transparency in Land Acquisition, Rehabilitation and Resettlement (Amendment) Bill, 2015' [1]. The reader may well accuse me of straying from the topic, not discussing the Bill at all, the individual clauses, the pros, the cons etc. I fully accept this critique...

However, I will say this... First what we need is a mindset change towards whole concept of land, its ownership, belonging, our related emotions, our resulting actions thereof etc. This book chiefly, in fact only, deals with this... First, we need to get our thoughts, our mindset in the 'right' place. Only then can and should we start debating the finer points of this Bill. I say this again, without a proper frame of mind, going into the subtleties of the Bill will be pointless, in fact may even be counterproductive.

So here is urging all to realize what is at stake... It is still not too late... I end with a Chinese proverb...

'The best time to plant a tree was 20 years ago. The second best time is now.' [44]

17. References

[1]   P. o. India, "THE RIGHT TO FAIR COMPENSATION AND
       TRANSPARENCY IN LAND ACQUISITION,
       REHABILITATION AND RESETTLEMENT
       (AMENDMENT) SECOND ORDINANCE, 2015," 2015.
       [Online]. Available:
       http://dolr.nic.in/dolr/downloads/pdfs/RFCTLARR%20Act%2
       0(Amendment)%20Second%20Ordinance,%202015.pdf.
       [Accessed 26 July 2015].

[2]   Wikipedia, "The Right to Fair Compensation and
       Transparency in Land Acquisition, Rehabilitation and
       Resettlement Act, 2013 --- Wikipedia, The Free
       Encyclopedia," 2015. [Online]. Available:
       http://en.wikipedia.org/w/index.php?title=The_Right_to_Fai
       r_Compensation_and_Transparency_in_Land_Acquisition,
       _Rehabilitation_and_Resettlement_Act,_2013&oldid=6655
       97508. [Accessed 9 June 2015].

[3]   A. Nashikkar and ors., "The Mumbai Pune Expressway: A
       Case study," 2000. [Online]. Available:
       http://www.iitk.ac.in/3inetwork/html/reports/IIMStudReport
       2000/mpecase1.pdf. [Accessed 26 July 2015].

[4]   H. Palshikar and H. Bhosale, "Order/Judgment Writ Petition
       WP/10/1997," 1997. [Online]. Available:

http://bombayhighcourt.nic.in. [Accessed 10 October 2015].

[5]   Wikipedia, "Bhakra Dam --- Wikipedia, The Free
        Encyclopedia," 2015. [Online]. Available:
        https://en.wikipedia.org/w/index.php?title=Bhakra_Dam&old
        id=683007189. [Accessed 10 October 2015].

[6]   P. M. Team, "Villagers protest against IIIT, claim loss of
        land," 2015. [Online]. Available:
        http://www.punemirror.in/pune/civic/Villagers-protest-
        against-IIIT-claim-loss-of-land/articleshow/47389093.cms.
        [Accessed 30 July 2015].

[7]   Wikipedia, "Anatomically modern humans --- Wikipedia,
        The Free Encyclopedia," 2015. [Online]. Available:
        http://en.wikipedia.org/w/index.php?title=Anatomically_mod
        ern_humans&oldid=664775873. [Accessed 12 June 2015].

[8]   Wikipedia, "Agroforestry --- Wikipedia, The Free
        Encyclopedia," 2015. [Online]. Available:
        http://en.wikipedia.org/w/index.php?title=Agroforestry&oldi
        d=662267927. [Accessed 12 June 2015].

[9]   S. Basu, "India opposes 2020 deadline for DDT ban," 2013.
        [Online]. Available:
        http://www.downtoearth.org.in/news/india-opposes-2020-
        deadline-for-ddt-ban-40967. [Accessed 10 October 2015].

[10]   Wikipedia, "Evolution --- Wikipedia, The Free
        Encyclopedia," 2015. [Online]. Available:
        https://en.wikipedia.org/w/index.php?title=Evolution&oldid=
        666470985. [Accessed 14 June 2015].

[11]   C. Sagan, Dragons of Eden: Speculations on the evolution of human intelligence, Ballantine Books, 2012.

[12]   Wikipedia, "Triune brain --- Wikipedia, The Free Encyclopedia," 2015. [Online]. Available: https://en.wikipedia.org/w/index.php?title=Triune_brain&old id=645850640. [Accessed 14 June 2015].

[13]   Wikipedia, "Maya (illusion) --- Wikipedia, The Free Encyclopedia," 2015. [Online]. Available: https://en.wikipedia.org/w/index.php?title=Maya_(illusion)&o ldid=660436788. [Accessed 21 June 2015].

[14]   Wikipedia, "Mahabharat (1988 TV series) --- Wikipedia, The Free Encyclopedia," 2015. [Online]. Available: https://en.wikipedia.org/w/index.php?title=Mahabharat_(198 8_TV_series)&oldid=666011027. [Accessed 21 June 2015].

[15]   L. Stevens, "Development: key to lasting peace," 2013. [Online]. Available: http://www.nationmultimedia.com/opinion/Development-key-to-lasting-peace-30215276.html. [Accessed 21 June 2015].

[16]   R. Team, "Things you must know about the Land Acquisition Bill," 2013. [Online]. Available: http://www.rediff.com/business/special/special-things-you-must-know-about-the-land-acquisition-bill/20130909.htm. [Accessed 29 September 2015].

[17]   Wikipedia, "Concurrent List --- Wikipedia, The Free Encyclopedia," 2015. [Online]. Available: https://en.wikipedia.org/w/index.php?title=Concurrent_List

&oldid=662894749. [Accessed 26 July 2015].

[18] D. Team, "Watch: Controversial Mumbai Development Plan 2034 scrapped by Maharashtra government," 2015. [Online]. Available: http://www.dnaindia.com/mumbai/report-controversial-mumbai-development-plan-2034-scrapped-by-maharashtra-government-2079293. [Accessed 26 July 2015].

[19] U. Govt., "US Debt Clock," 2015. [Online]. Available: http://www.usdebtclock.org. [Accessed 24 August 2015].

[20] Wikipedia, "BRIC --- Wikipedia, The Free Encyclopedia," 2015. [Online]. Available: https://en.wikipedia.org/w/index.php?title=BRIC&oldid=674639775. [Accessed 24 August 2015].

[21] Wikipedia, "World population --- Wikipedia, The Free Encyclopedia," 2015. [Online]. Available: https://en.wikipedia.org/w/index.php?title=World_population&oldid=677438317. [Accessed 24 August 2015].

[22] Wikipedia, "China–Pakistan relations --- Wikipedia, The Free Encyclopedia," 2015. [Online]. Available: https://en.wikipedia.org/w/index.php?title=China%E2%80%93Pakistan_relations&oldid=673571345. [Accessed 27 August 2015].

[23] T. N. Team, "Xi sees Pakistan becoming Asian Tiger," 2015. [Online]. Available: http://nation.com.pk/national/22-Apr-2015/xi-sees-pakistan-becoming-asian-tiger. [Accessed 27 August 2015].

[24] Wikipedia, "Xinjiang conflict --- Wikipedia, The Free
      Encyclopedia," 2015. [Online]. Available:
      https://en.wikipedia.org/w/index.php?title=Xinjiang_conflict
      &oldid=677617444. [Accessed 27 August 2015].

[25] Wikipedia, "Pakistan and state-sponsored terrorism ---
      Wikipedia, The Free Encyclopedia," 2015. [Online].
      Available:
      https://en.wikipedia.org/w/index.php?title=Pakistan_and_stat
      e-sponsored_terrorism&oldid=677333843. [Accessed 27
      August 2015].

[26] A. Kingsbury, "Why China Helped Countries Like Pakistan,
      North Korea Build Nuclear Bombs," 2009. [Online].
      Available:
      http://www.usnews.com/news/world/articles/2009/01/02/wh
      y-china-helped-countries-like-pakistan-north-korea-build-
      nuclear-bombs. [Accessed 27 August 2015].

[27] W. Burr, "China, Pakistan, and the Bomb: The Declassified
      File on U.S. Policy, 1977-1997; National Security Archive
      Electronic Briefing Book No. 114," 2004. [Online].
      Available: http://nsarchive.gwu.edu/NSAEBB/NSAEBB114.
      [Accessed 27 August 2015].

[28] J. Norbu, "Who Created Pakistan's Nuclear Arsenal?," 2011.
      [Online]. Available: http://www.huffingtonpost.com/jamyang-
      norbu/who-created-pakistans-
      nuc_b_864124.html?ir=India&adsSiteOverride=in.
      [Accessed 27 August 2015].

[29] W. Team, "China's Nuclear Warning," 2015. [Online].

Available: http://www.wsj.com/articles/chinas-nuclear-warning-1429831422. [Accessed 27 August 2015].

[30] T. Weiner, "NUCLEAR ANXIETY: THE KNOW-HOW," 1998. [Online]. Available: http://www.nytimes.com/1998/06/01/world/nuclear-anxiety-the-know-how-us-and-china-helped-pakistan-build-its-bomb.html. [Accessed 27 August 2015].

[31] Wikipedia, "Nasr (missile) --- Wikipedia, The Free Encyclopedia," 2015. [Online]. Available: https://en.wikipedia.org/w/index.php?title=Nasr_(missile)&oldid=673955210. [Accessed 27 August 2015].

[32] R. Fisher Jr., "Pakistan's Long Range Ballistic Missiles: A View From IDEAS," 2004. [Online]. Available: http://www.strategycenter.net/research/pubID.47/pub_detail.asp. [Accessed 27 August 2015].

[33] I. News, "IDN TAKE: The Farce that is Shaheen III," 2015. [Online]. Available: http://www.indiandefensenews.in/2015/03/idn-take-farce-of-shaeen-iii.html. [Accessed 27 August 2015].

[34] C. f. N. Studies, "China's Missile Exports and Assistance to Pakistan - Statements and Developments," 1999. [Online]. Available: http://cns.miis.edu/archive/country_india/china/mpakchr.htm. [Accessed 27 August 2015].

[35] V. K. Nair, "THE CHINESE THREAT: AN INDIAN PERSPECTIVE," 2003. [Online]. Available: http://www.jamestown.org/programs/chinabrief/single/?tx_tt

news%5Btt_news%5D=3763&tx_ttnews%5BbackPid%5D=1
91&no_cache=1#.VdwSSP7os2w. [Accessed 27 August
2015].

[36] Wikipedia, "String of Pearls (Indian Ocean) --- Wikipedia,
      The Free Encyclopedia," 2015. [Online]. Available:
      https://en.wikipedia.org/w/index.php?title=String_of_Pearls_
      (Indian_Ocean)&oldid=670092781. [Accessed 4 September
      2015].

[37] R. Srinivasan, "The existential threat to India posed by
      China's Pakistan gambit," 2015. [Online]. Available:
      http://www.firstpost.com/world/existential-threat-india-
      posed-chinas-pakistan-gambit-2226726.html. [Accessed 5
      September 2015].

[38] B. Chellaney, "A silk glove for China's iron fist," 2015.
      [Online]. Available:
      http://www.taipeitimes.com/News/editorials/archives/2015/
      03/06/2003612863/2. [Accessed 5 September 2015].

[39] Wikipedia, "List of countries by military expenditures ---
      Wikipedia, The Free Encyclopedia," 2015. [Online].
      Available:
      https://en.wikipedia.org/w/index.php?title=List_of_countries
      _by_military_expenditures&oldid=682411278. [Accessed
      28 September 2015].

[40] B. I. Team, "108 Giant Chinese Infrastructure Projects That
      Are Reshaping The World," 2015. [Online]. Available:
      http://www.businessinsider.com/108-giant-chinese-
      infrastructure-projects-that-are-reshaping-the-world-2011-

12?IR=T. [Accessed 24 August 2015].

[41] c. Blogger, "List of Super engineering," 2015. [Online].
      Available:
      http://blog.sina.com.cn/s/blog_5a53af350100ao0k.html.
      [Accessed 24 August 2015].

[42] R. Singhal, "India-China Deficit: Beyond Iron Ore," 2015.
      [Online]. Available: http://thediplomat.com/2015/06/india-
      china-deficit-beyond-iron-ore. [Accessed 10 October 2015].

[43] Wikipedia, "Liu Xiaobo --- Wikipedia, The Free
      Encyclopedia," 2015. [Online]. Available:
      https://en.wikipedia.org/w/index.php?title=Liu_Xiaobo&oldi
      d=666318221. [Accessed 6 August 2015].

[44] N. Kuechler, "Favorite Quotes: Chinese Proverb on the
      Best Time to Plant a Tree," 2006. [Online]. Available:
      http://nicholaskuechler.com/2006/10/23/favorite-quotes-
      chinese-proverb-best-time-to-plant-a-tree. [Accessed 30
      September 2015].

www.ingramcontent.com/pod-product-compliance
Lightning Source LLC
Chambersburg PA
CBHW050414290526
45786CB00003B/1253